Fiji Islands
we spent time
LABASA
ANUA
EVU
SAVU SAVU
Rabi
Kioa
Laucala
Qamea
Taveuni
Naitauba
Vanua
Balavu
Yacata
Koro
Mago
Lau Group
Nairai
Gau
Cicia
Nayau
Lakeba
Moala
Totoya
Matuku
SAN FRANCISCO
HONOLULU
LOS ANGELES
ACAPULCO
GILBERT
ELLICE
HONIARA
SANTO
VILA
APIA
PAGO
PAGO
PAPEETE
FIJI
RAROTONGA
NOUMEA
TONGA
Pacific Ocean
SYDNEY
AUCKLAND

FIJI SKETCHBOOK

The Sketchbook Series

SYDNEY SKETCHBOOK
Drawings by Unk White
Text by Tess van Sommers

ADELAIDE SKETCHBOOK
Drawings by Jeanette McLeod
Text by Max Lamshed

BRISBANE SKETCHBOOK
Drawings by Unk White
Text by Peter Newell

NORTHERN TERRITORY SKETCHBOOK
Drawings by Ainslie Roberts
Text by Douglas Lockwood

CANBERRA SKETCHBOOK
Drawings by Unk White
Text by Peter Luck

BAROSSA VALLEY SKETCHBOOK
Drawings by Jeanette McLeod
Text by Colin Thiele

CHRISTCHURCH SKETCHBOOK
Drawings by Unk White
Text by M. H. Holcroft

WELLINGTON SKETCHBOOK
Drawings by Unk White
Text by M. H. Holcroft

GOLD COAST SKETCHBOOK
Drawings by Kevin Jopson
Text by Peter Newell

RIVER MURRAY SKETCHBOOK
Drawings by Jeanette McLeod
Text by Ian Mudie

W.A. GOLDFIELDS SKETCHBOOK
Drawings by Arthur Evan Read
Text by Kim Lockwood

HAWKESBURY RIVER SKETCHBOOK
Drawings by Unk White
Text by Frank Cayley

THE ROCKS, SYDNEY
Drawings by Unk White
Text by Olaf Ruhen

MELBOURNE SKETCHBOOK
Drawings by Unk White
Text by W. H. Newnham

PERTH SKETCHBOOK
Drawings by Paul Rigby
Text by Kirwan Ward

HOBART SKETCHBOOK
Drawings by Max Angus
Text by Patsy Adam Smith

NEWCASTLE SKETCHBOOK
Drawings by Unk White
Text by Alan Farrelly

NORFOLK ISLAND SKETCHBOOK
Drawings by Unk White
Text by Ruth Sriber

AUCKLAND SKETCHBOOK
Drawings by Unk White
Text by M. H. Holcroft

BROKEN HILL SKETCHBOOK
Drawings by Frank Beck
Text by Donald McLean

SYDNEY HARBOUR SKETCHBOOK
Drawings by Unk White
Text by Charles Sriber

ROTTNEST ISLAND SKETCHBOOK
Drawings by Paul Rigby
Text by Kirwan Ward

BURRA SKETCHBOOK
Drawings by Maurice Perry
Text by Ian Auhl

NEW ENGLAND SKETCHBOOK
Drawings by Unk White
Text by Peter Newell

BENDIGO SKETCHBOOK
Drawings by Unk White
Text by John Béchervaise

In preparation

BLUE MOUNTAINS SKETCHBOOK
GRAMPIANS SKETCHBOOK
BALLARAT SKETCHBOOK
PORT PHILLIP BAY SKETCHBOOK
ADELAIDE HILLS SKETCHBOOK
ALICE SPRINGS SKETCHBOOK
PADDINGTON SKETCHBOOK
PARRAMATTA SKETCHBOOK
NORTH ADELAIDE SKETCHBOOK
PORT MACQUARIE SKETCHBOOK
NORTH QUEENSLAND SKETCHBOOK
FIJI SKETCHBOOK
VICTOR HARBOUR SKETCHBOOK
TASMANIA SKETCHBOOK
GEELONG SKETCHBOOK
DARWIN SKETCHBOOK
DARLING DOWNS SKETCHBOOK
WESTERN DISTRICT SKETCHBOOK
DANDENONGS SKETCHBOOK
PORT ARTHUR SKETCHBOOK

Ida Mae Steck's Fiji March 1975

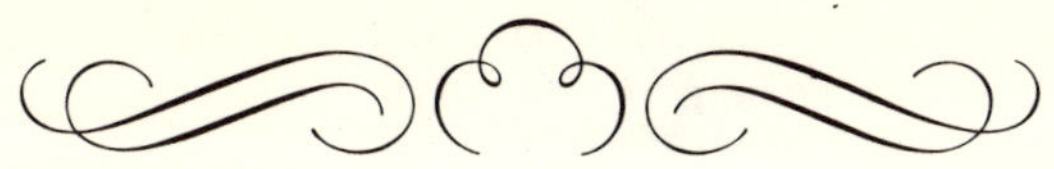

FIJI SKETCHBOOK

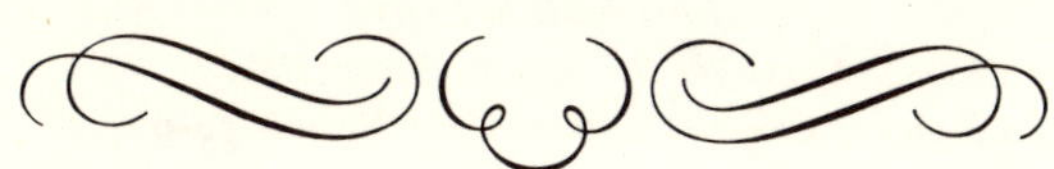

VICTOR DOVE

with most regards
Victor Dove

RIGBY LIMITED

RIGBY LIMITED • ADELAIDE • SYDNEY
MELBOURNE • BRISBANE • PERTH

First published 1970

Library of Congress Catalog Card Number 74-98416
National Library of Australia Card Number & ISBN 0 85179 028 3

Wholly designed and set up in Australia
Printed by Toppan Printing Co. (H.K.) Ltd, Hong Kong

CONTENTS

Above: *Basket-making in Suva Market*

FIJIAN PRONUNCIATION

In this book, the accepted Fijian method of spelling has been used throughout. The Fijian language is completely phonetic, unlike English in which, for example, C can be pronounced as either a K or an S. In Fijian, D is always sounded as ND, so that Nadi is pronounced Nandi. B is always MB, so Labasa is pronounced Lambasa. C is sounded as TH, so Cakobau becomes Thakombau. G is sounded as NG, so that Sigatoka is pronounced as Singatoka. And Q is sounded like the NG in "finger." So the name Beqa has the B sounded as MB, and the Q sounded as NG, and is pronounced Mbenga. Generally the emphasis is on the last syllable but one of each word. Korolevu, for example, should be pronounced Koro-LE-VU.

LAW OF THE CLUB

When King Cakobau of Fiji gave the islands to Queen Victoria, he sent her "his old and favourite war-club." In a letter which accompanied the horrid weapon, he said that the war-club had once been the only known law of Fiji. "Many of the people, whole tribes, died and passed away under the old law," he wrote, "but hundreds of thousands still survive to learn and enjoy the better state of things."

The war-club had ruled Fiji for centuries, since the days of the Oceanic migrations. It is believed that the forebears of the Fijians were among the peoples who moved eastwards from Malaysia and Indonesia to populate New Guinea and other Melanesian islands. Once settled in the islands, they began a centuries-long process of intermingling with such nearby island races as the Samoans and Tongans.

After occupying the islands now known as Fiji, from a corruption of the name of the main island of Viti Levu, the migrant race settled down to establish themselves as the most fearsome seagoing warriors of the Pacific. In 1777, Captain Cook saw some Fijians at Tonga, and remarked that "the Feegee men were much respected . . . not only from the power and cruel manner of their nation's going to war but also from their ingenuity."

Cook referred to the Fijian weapons, which were strongly made and artistically decorated, and to the tapa cloth and basketwork of the type which is still woven by nimble Fijian fingers, and sells in great quantities to the tourists.

But in those days, the weapons were the most significant artifacts, and the Fijians used them with a ferocious skill. A peculiar horror of Fijian warfare was that prisoners were ritually slain, cooked in earth ovens, and eaten with great gusto. There is a tendency to play down this part of the Fijian past, and to state that only a few people were eaten so that those who dined upon them might absorb their peculiar qualities of courage or wisdom. The accounts of early missionaries and adventurers, however, leave little doubt that the Fijians ate human beings simply because they liked the taste. Anthropologists say that the custom may have developed from human sacrifice—the eating of food offered to the gods—or because human flesh was the readiest source of protein on islands which lacked other large animals.

Nor did they confine themselves to eating those from other islands. The Fijian tribes carried on a complicated warfare amongst themselves, and seem to have regarded it as something like a sport. Apart from regional jealousies, they used quite petty incidents as excuses for wars in which every participant was well aware that he stood a good chance of ending as the focal point of a cannibal feast.

Because the effectiveness of their weapons was limited to the strength of a human arm, the balance of power between the tribes remained about even until the coming of the white man, which was in the early years of last century. Before then, Fiji had had little attraction for traders or explorers. Abel Tasman touched at the islands in 1643, and

Fijian Warrior

Captain Cook sighted them but wisely decided to steer clear. After Captain Bligh was cast adrift by the *Bounty* mutineers he passed close to the Yasawa group, and saw canoes coming out to chase him, but he had sailed with Cook and knew that the open sea held fewer terrors than a Fijian beach. A few ships had contact with the islands, but usually suffered from the experience.

Greed, as always, proved stronger than fear, and in this case the greed was for sandalwood. When it became known that the islands were a prolific source of this sweet-smelling timber, a number of traders took tremendous chances for the sake of the huge profits. A cargo obtained in exchange for a few paltry trade goods could be sold for thousands of pounds.

Within a few years the islands were so robbed of the tree that a specimen is now hard to find, and in the process the traders destroyed the fine balance of Fijian power. The man who was most to blame for this was called Charles Savage; a seaman from the American brig *Eliza* which was wrecked off Nairai Island in 1805.

Amongst her cargo was a quantity of muskets and ammunition, and Savage took some of these to the island of Bau. He enlisted with the chief, taught his warriors how to use the firearms, and gathered together a group of European mercenaries which may have included some escaped convicts from Australia.

The new weapons meant that a tribe without them was helpless, and by the time Charles Savage was killed, in 1813, many more warriors had obtained firearms. Helped by white adventurers, they battled with each other even more determinedly than before, but the island of Bau, which had been first to obtain muskets, gradually gained ascendancy. Cakobau, the grand-nephew of the chief for whom Charles Savage had fought, emerged as the strong man of the islands.

With his law of the club he imposed some kind of unity upon the tribes, but he still clung to the savage old traditions. Widows were strangled on the grave of their husband, and Cakobau performed this service for his own father. When a

chief's house was built, a slave was buried alive in the hole dug for each of the main poles. Old people were killed to put them out of their misery, offenders were swung round by the legs and had their brains bashed out against a rock, and human flesh was still the most relished source of protein.

Into this barbaric kingdom, in 1835, came two men whose courage and devotion were to begin the long process of leading the inhabitants to "learn and enjoy the better state of things." They were the missionaries William Cross and David Cargill who, despite the threats and derision of the islanders, were to plant the seed of a faith which has grown as strongly as that of the raintree, whose seeds were brought to Fiji by later missionaries.

Nowadays, when seeing the smiling and neatly-dressed groups which stream into the Methodist churches on Sunday mornings, it is difficult to realize that their ancestors held cannibal orgies outside the houses of the first missionaries, in an attempt to frighten them away. One, the Reverend Thomas Baker, met the traditional fate of missionaries when he was eaten in 1867. His charred shoes may be seen in Suva Museum . . . not far from the great wooden

forks and spoons which were used for serving human flesh.

But Cross and Cargill, together with a few Tonga Christians from the mission on that island, refused to give up their task. When the Deed of Cession was signed, the British emissary, Sir Hercules Robinson, said, "The great social advantages which have been made during the last forty years from savage heathenism are due to the self-denying and unostentatious labours of the Wesleyan Church."

The missionaries did not only have to combat the savagery of the Fijians. Another of their problems was that of the white men who were trading with the islanders, and who were enjoying a good thing which they did not care to see upset by the preachers. About thirty of them, including the descendants of convicts who had escaped from Australia, had settled at Levuka, on the island of Ovalau. They married Fijian women, and developed a trade in such island products as turtle-shell, which in pre-plastics days was valued for the making of hair-combs and other toilet-ware.

Levuka thus became the first permanent settlement of the intruders upon the islands, and was to grow into the centre of commerce and administration (or maladministration) until Cakobau gave the islands to the British and a new capital was established at Suva. Now, it is a little town which straggles along a shelf of coastline at the foot of steep mountains—so steep that each level of the township was connected by huge flights of steps instead of streets. Many of the old houses have gone, and the town seems to snuggle into the mountainside as though dreaming of its tumultuous past. The flights of steps remain, though some of them come to an abrupt conclusion in dense tangles of undergrowth, and there is an atmosphere of romantic neglect which would make the town a fitting background for one of Somerset Maugham's stories about the South Seas. The Royal Hotel, an old wooden building which seems to sway as gently as an anchored lugger when the wind storms in from the sea, hints at forgotten tales of the days when there were scores of bars along Levuka waterfront, and a shipmaster could find his way into port "by following the gin-bottles drifting out to sea."

The missionaries opened a school for the children of Levuka, in a first attempt to drive a wedge between the settlers and their Godless ways. But the way of the missionaries was to be long and hard, and the faith and courage with which they continued their task must call for the utmost admiration.

Unimpressed by such missionary efforts as the compiling of a Fijian dictionary and the establishment of churches and schools, Cakobau continued to enjoy his seven wives, his cannibal orgies, and an eleven years' war with the Rewa tribe. Firearms had injected a new element into Fijian warfare, and the chiefs converted their canoes into more effective fighting craft by fitting them with small cannons. This facilitated their invasion of neighbouring islands, because they could blast a mob of warriors off the beaches instead of laying off shore and exchanging ritual insults and a shower of spears and throwing-clubs.

Cynics say that the slow progress of Cakobau's war with Rewa opened his mind to the exhortations of the missionaries. In 1854 he was converted to Christianity, and as an immediate bonus received an alliance with King George of Tonga, who was also a Christian. Tongan warriors had played a part in Fijian politics for many years, and a Fijian chief who found himself unable to subdue the opposition by using his own men was apt to hire a group of Tongans to do the job for him. King George brought an army to Fiji, and helped Cakobau to conquer the Rewa and make himself Chief of Western Fiji. The eastern half was governed by Ma'afu, a nephew of King George.

Perhaps "governed" is too definite a word to apply to the administration of Fiji in that era, for the white settlers enjoyed an anarchic situation in which they carried on their own small wars, especially against the Lovoni tribe in the Levuka area, and which enabled them to negotiate the purchase of land almost on their own terms. Fijian land was technically the communal property of the tribes who lived upon it, but it was impossible for the chiefs to resist the lure of trade goods—and especially that of the teeth of the sperm whales. These were regarded as particularly sacred objects, and even nowadays can be seen on sale in Chinese and Indian stores.

Most prominent of the land-dealers was John Williams, the U.S. Vice-Consul, who bought large parcels of land, including a complete island, for the equivalent of about twenty dollars in modern Australian currency. He built a two-storied house on his island and proceeded to celebrate the Fourth of July, but his pyrotechnics set the house on fire. A crowd of Fijians, gathered to watch the fun, moved in on the fire, and looted the burning house. Their action began more than twenty years of trouble for Chief Cakobau.

Filled with righteous indignation, Williams complained to his government. He asked it to collect damages for him, but not much was done until 1855. In that year the exasperated Lovoni tribe raided and burnt Levuka, and the property of a number of American citizens went up in flames. Perhaps inspired by their example, other Fijians set fire to another house which Williams had built.

This time, Williams complained to such effect that the U.S. Government sent a frigate from Samoa. Cakobau was summoned aboard, and threatened into signing a promise to pay $18,000.

This piece of gunboat diplomacy was continued in 1858, when another U.S. warship appeared. Her captain demanded that Cakobau should surrender either himself or the money, but by this time Cakobau had another card to play. He offered the islands to Great Britain, on condition that Britain should pay his debt to the United States.

His offer was taken to Britain by the first British Consul, who had recently settled in Levuka. It contained various terms which were not acceptable to the British Government, but it took four years for the offer to be declined. In what seems like a gesture of desperation, Cakobau then tried to give his islands to the United States. But by that time Congress was involved in fighting the Civil War, and did not even bother to answer him.

As the years went by, Cakobau may have thought that the debt was forgotten, but governments have long memories, In 1867, a third American warship appeared, and her captain threatened to bombard Levuka if Cakobau did not pay up. The Chief signed yet another IOU, though he had

Hibiscus

Road in Suva

no more hope of raising the money than before. His Fijian subjects rarely handled cash, and the white settlers would have regarded any attempt to tax them as sheer impudence.

News of Cakobau's predicament was freely discussed around the Pacific, and it came at last to the ears of the U.S. Consul in Melbourne. This gentleman hit upon a neat and businesslike solution. He approached a group of Melbourne financiers, and suggested that they should offer to pay off Cakobau's debt in exchange for 200,000 acres of land. The financiers formed an organization which they called the Polynesian Company (despite the fact that Fiji is in Melanesia, not Polynesia) and sent an envoy to Cakobau. Although he did not own the land, Cakobau signed the company's charter.

The company moved in and took up the first of their land around the present site of Suva, and established a sugar plantation. With nostalgic optimism they christened the area Toorak, and possibly hoped that it would soon become as desirable as the Melbourne suburb of that name. But the inexperienced planters failed to make a success of their crop, and what cane they did deliver to the mill was spoiled by amateur millers. The plantation was reclaimed by the jungle, and Toorak is now the seediest suburb of Suva.

Cakobau's most pressing problem had been solved, but another one soon arose. The first offer of cession to Great Britain, with its implied possibility of a stable administration, had attracted a number of Australian and European settlers to the islands. Most of these were simply in search of easy pickings, and faded away when they found that the islanders were still liable to fall back upon spears and war-clubs as an aid to negotiations. But a hard core of solid settlers remained, and this community slowly increased. Intent upon the peaceful accumulation of wealth, the settlers deplored the still comparatively lawless state of the islands. They pressed Cakobau to do something about it, and in 1865 the Confederacy of Independent Kingdoms was formed. But the

Fijian woman making baskets

various tribal chiefs, who only a short time before would have regarded each other as collections of tasty joints, could not work together. The Confederacy collapsed, and Cakobau was not having much more success in controlling the turbulent chiefs in his own half of the island.

It seemed that the "law of the club" might be the only one which the islanders would obey, so the settlers took matters into their own hands. In 1871, some of them proclaimed that Cakobau was King of Fiji and head of its "legal government." But other settlers scoffed at the idea, and Cakobau's kingdom was little more than a name.

So the ageing chief decided, for the third time, that the best way to solve his problems was to give his country away.

In 1872, he asked for German protection. Fortunately for the British, since Fiji would have made a superb Pacific base for the German Navy, his offer was rejected by Chancellor Bismarck.

In 1874, Cakobau approached Britain again, and this time his offer was accepted. Sir Hercules Robinson, the Governor of New South Wales, went to Fiji to negotiate the Deed of Cession, and it was signed on 10 October 1874 by Cakobau, "styled Tui Viti and Vuni Valu," and by twelve more "high Chiefs of the said islands."

For such an important instrument, the Deed is remarkably short. It contains less than 2,000 words, and its language is agreeably crisp and clear. One of its seven clauses is of

Suva waterfront

particular significance, because it states in part that, "all questions of financial liabilities and engagements shall be carefully scrutinized, and dealt with upon the principles of justice and sound public policy."

This may have been aimed at the Polynesian Company, whose claims to the land which it had purchased for nine cents an acre were firmly rejected by the new Crown Colony. However, the government did repay the money spent on settling Cakobau's debt to the U.S.A., and, when it was decided that the new capital should be established at Suva, the company was compensated for the loss of its overgrown plantation.

New Central building, Victoria Parade Suva

This was not until 1882, when the government decided that Levuka was too cramped, exposed, and isolated to be a suitable capital. One of the reasons for choosing Suva as the capital was the magnificent harbour, even though the planners could not have visualized the giant liners which now sail through the gap in its protective coral reef (which is slowly being eaten alive by the Crown of Thorns starfish) and tie up in deep water alongside King's Wharf, only a few minutes from the main business centre.

The harbour is no less magnificent in the scenic sense. To the north and west, it is enclosed by hills as steep and irregular as the sea after a hurricane, and they are almost smothered by a green foam of jungle. Here and there, as they tumble westwards towards the hazy distances of the horizon, the basic rock breaks through. It is grey, stark, and rugged; a reminder that the Fiji Islands are the peaks of a huge mountain range which is hidden in the depths of the Pacific. Some of the peaks are oddly shaped, like that which is called

Chinese Stall
Suva

Suva Market

the Thumb because its backward-curving angle resembles a gargantuan thumb protruding through the dense jungle green.

This green is repeated on the five islands of the Bay of Islands, also in the west of the harbour. They are small—one of them so small that it was cutely christened Honeymoon Island, because it is "just big enough for two"—and resemble huge bouquets of foliage adrift on the placid water.

The busiest part of the town is the wharf area. Behind it, the suburban roofs are scattered amongst the thickly-forested hills and ridges, and to the westward there is a small commercial complex of warehouses and oil-tanks before the metropolitan area peters out in a sprinkling of bungalows along the spurs of the ranges. The wharves accommodate ships which range down from the huge cruise-liners to Japanese tuna-fishing craft, decorated with a frieze of sharks' tails which the crews are taking home to sell as

Fijian Sentry

delicacies. The prison, which bears a vague resemblance to a Foreign Legion fort, stands to the west of the wharf area. It was once said that the worst punishment which the warders could inflict upon a Fijian prisoner was to lock him outside for the night.

East of the wharves, a façade of business and administrative buildings faces the harbour. They include a new motel in the familiar modern American and Australian style, and some of the other new buildings are in that characterless combination of steel, glass, and cement which will shortly make every city in the world resemble all the others.

A redevelopment and reclamation scheme is changing the face of the waterfront, and many old landmarks are disappearing. This modernization is being accompanied by a quickening in the tempo, and the traditional easygoing South Sea Islands charm may eventually be replaced by a glossier and more brittle image . . . at least in the centre of the town. There are new shopping arcades, supermarkets, and offices, and the narrow streets are experiencing traffic problems.

The seaborne traveller's introduction to the commercial world of Suva is likely to be at the Municipal Market. This stands behind King's Wharf, and gives the market vendors first option on the newcomers before they can reach the shops. The market stalls are a magnetic conglomeration of baskets, grass skirts, coral necklaces, straw mats, tapa cloth, shell jewellery; and masks, bowls, images, and furniture carved out of raintree wood. Like most other shopkeepers in Fiji, the stallholders are perfectly prepared to bargain, and would be astonished if anyone paid their first asking price.

Superficially, most of Suva's trade seems to be aimed at the tourist, and a host of shops are stocked with duty-free goods such as transistors and tape-recorders. But the streets which hold them can soon be left behind. Side roads, leading off Victoria Parade, meander away to pleasant avenues of old colonial homes, standing in quiet gardens which are brilliant with hibiscus, poinsettia, and frangipani. The streets rising sharply behind the town all wind through a kind of tropical suburbia, and some of the homes have a suburban neatness which is somehow mocked at by the explosive greenery of gardens looking as though constant vigilance is needed to prevent them from taking over the whole establishment. Other houses are slaphappy constructions of timber and corrugated iron, and these appear to have come to terms with the writhing coils of vegetation which festoon broken fences and sagging porches.

East of the town is Albert Park, which had a brief moment of fame when Sir Charles Kingsford Smith landed there in the *Southern Cross*, when he was pioneering the first Pacific air route in 1928. This part of Suva also contains the Domain, which must be the type of suburb envisaged by the Polynesian Company when they gave the name of Toorak to a forested hillside. The Domain stands on the slopes beyond Government House, and gazes aloofly out across the harbour and the broad Pacific. It is less than a century since Cakobau despairingly described the white men in Fiji as "mere stalkers on the beach . . . cormorants who will open their mouths and swallow us," but in that time the island has developed a social élite whose status is based upon the commercial or administrative success of the families of which it is constructed. Some of them live in the fine homes of the Domain, appropriately close to Government House, which is a splendid building in the colonial-residency style and approached by an avenue of palms. Its gates are guarded by a fiercely proud soldier who marches to and fro with his back as rigid as his own bayonet; his sulu as immaculately

Victoria Parade, Suva

white as the surf breaking on the reef and his red tunic as brilliant as a hibiscus flower.

Not far from Government House is the Grand Pacific Hotel, which like the Raffles Hotel in Singapore was once the haunt of empire-builders. Now, its dusky-pink walls and new air-conditioned wing shelter tourists travelling on package-deals from Texas, Auckland, and Wollongong.

The atmosphere of Suva has been described as "cosmopolitan," but despite the avid commercialism of its few crowded streets of shops, and the variety of languages and accents to be heard, it still retains an easygoing cheerfulness which is essentially that which is thought of as belonging to the "South Seas." If you smile at a Fijian, he will smile back, immediately and widely, and is instantly ready for a gossip which is generally free from any mendicant motive. Like businessmen anywhere, the Indian shopkeepers are alert to the possibility of making a sale, but they are usually gentle and dignified people whose "hard sell" is delivered in almost caressing tones, and who give a smiling shrug if they fail to close the deal. Above all, the people of Suva retain that responsive interest in other people which finds it hard to survive in the concrete anthills of western culture. It is a village quality, inherited from the days when people were more important than things, and it has not yet been swamped under the flood of duty-free goods which pours into Suva out of the holds of Japanese ships, and pours out again in the luggage of tourists. Its survival gives to Suva an atmosphere that is warm, earthy, and friendly, with a humanity as broad as a Fijian smile.

YAQONA AND MEKES

Some Fijian women can call turtles out of the sea. Some Fijian men can walk barefooted over a pit full of stones heated to such a degree that a handkerchief dropped upon them will burst into flames. There is no scientific explanation for either of these phenomena, and the Fijians account for them by saying that they are magical gifts, bestowed upon certain tribes by legendary figures of the past.

Fijian folklore is rich and strange, and the Fijians are a people who value traditions and ceremonies. Some of these may be of Polynesian origin, because Fiji is the frontier between Melanesia and Polynesia. It is the most easterly of the Melanesian Islands, which include Papua and New Guinea, and the Fijians are believed to have arrived from New Guinea by an island-hopping process which ended about eight thousand years ago. It is certain that they retained some Melanesian characteristics, especially that of intertribal warfare, and their massive bodies and strong features give evidence of a Melanesian strain.

But Polynesia is not far away. The people of Tonga are Polynesians, and for centuries there was a vigorous interplay of war, trade, and migration between the two groups of islands. The Tongans were noted for their great war-canoes, which the Fijians coveted and then imitated, and Tongan invaders settled on various Fijian islands. It is said that the families of principal Fijian chiefs are descended from such Polynesian invaders.

Whatever their racial origins may be, and however much they may have intermarried with other races, the Fijians are certainly splendid physical types—a fact which must have added to their warlike reputation. Both men and women are tall and heavily built, with thick necks, large features, and

Fijian Faces
Boy from Yasawa Islands
Paula, Beachcomber Hotel Fiji
Theresia from Taneuni Island
Maria (Rotuma)
Langsefura Rotuma
Polynesian from Rotuma
Kitioni Bagasau of Rewa
Japan

big, muscular arms and legs. Their skins are a dark brown, and their hair can grow into huge black frizzy mops—though nowadays it is usually neatly trimmed.

Their physical splendour is matched by lively intelligence, manual dexterity, and a strong sense of rhythm and design. These qualities, influenced by their love of tradition and ceremony, are manifested in their art, dances, and rituals.

Captain Cook spoke of seeing a "beautifully chequered cloth" which was of Fijian origin, and this must have been tapa, or masi, a fabric made from the inner bark of trees. It has a creamy colour, and on this background the Fijians imprint formal designs with dyes made from earth and plants, though nowadays there is a tendency to use a debased silk-screening process, and dyes out of tins. Tapa cloth was worn wrapped around the body like a bulky kilt, and was the forerunner of the modern sulu; a trimly-tailored kilt-like garment. For soldiers and police, the sulu hem is cut into a saw-toothed pattern, but civilians wear it with a plain hem.

Fijian basketwork is strong, well finished, and attractively designed. It is a true handicraft, and in some places a visitor can take delivery of basketware straight from the fingers of the woman who has just secured the last strand of cane. The traditional Fijian houses, called bures, also demonstrate this skill in weaving with the locally-obtainable fibres. The framework is built from forest timbers, bound together with sennit ropes. The walls are made of interwoven bamboo, and the ridged roof is thatched with palm fronds or pandanus leaves. The result is a sturdy structure; naturally air-conditioned and ideal for the climate. The interiors may be decorated with tapa cloth, and the earthen floors covered with finely plaited mats.

A chief's bure is usually a larger, high-roofed building set above the rest of the village on a platform of coral rocks. In the old days, the great main timbers would be richly carved—and set upon the skeleton of a slave or prisoner who had been buried alive.

The Fijian talent for woodcarving may also be glimpsed in the bowls, trays, salad-servers, ceremonial masks, coffee

Fijian Nurses, School of Medicine, Suva

tables, and statuettes, all made from the wood of the raintree or monkey-pod tree. Huge quantities of these are sold to tourists, but they are all so exactly alike that they are obviously turned out on lathes and jigsaws. They lack the individuality of the carvings which can be seen in the museum, especially on the war-clubs which once made the Fijians the terror of their neighbours.

Especial skill is devoted to the carving of the large wooden bowls, standing on stumpy legs, which are used for the ceremonial serving of yaqona, or kava. This is the traditional drink of welcome for a distinguished guest, and the yaqona ceremony is carried out according to rituals whose dignity and solemnity reflects the Fijian love for tradition.

In the past, this tradition required that yaqona should

always be freshly made from the pounded green roots of *Piper methysticum*, a shrub which is a member of the pepper family. Nowadays, the rhythmic thump of a mechanical yaqona pounder can be heard from a shed near the Suva waterfront, and the powder is sold in packets.

The author participated in a yaqona ceremony in the village long-house at Yalobi, on Waya Island in the Yasawa Group. The guests were seated in three rows, and the Fijians were in two groups on either side of the yanggona bowl. All the men were dressed in the traditional meke costume of grass skirts and leaves, ornamented with flowers of the flamboyant trees. A short rope of coconut fibre, ornamented with cowrie shells, led towards the chief guest, and in the old days this was guarded by two club-carrying warriors whose duty was to kill anyone who crossed the rope.

The crushed yaqona root was mixed with water in the bowl, and strained through a bundle of hibiscus fibres, while the chief delivered an oration punctuated by deep sighs from the assembled warriors. When the mixture was ready, an attendant brought half a coconut-shell to be filled, then turned and carried it to the chief guest, advancing in the traditional half-crouching posture and with outstretched arms. In accordance with the ritual, the guest clapped hands once, took the cup and drained it in one swallow, and then sent it spinning back over the floor-mats towards the bowl, clapping his hands three times. The same ceremony was

Presenting the Yagona

followed by every member of the party, while the warriors clapped hands in unison with the guests and chanted the ancient songs.

The yaqona itself resembles a weak mixture of chocolate and water, and has a slightly medicinal flavour not unlike a cough mixture. It is not alcoholic, but those who have drunk enough yaqona report that it has a strangely paralytic effect on the legs. This wears off, but the drink leaves no hangover.

The costume worn at the yaqona ceremony is the same as that worn during mekes; the Fijian art of the dance. With men, this has an essentially martial character, and like the dances of most primitive peoples it was once used to preserve, in a stylised form, the history and traditions of the race. In mime and song, the dancers re-enact the legendary battles, victories, and adventures of their tribe, and in the old days such dances would be performed before combat; with the dual purpose of reminding the warriors of past glories and whipping up the fighting-spirit anew.

A war-dance is a dramatic spectacle. It is performed to a fast, erratic rhythm provided by the clapping of hands, the beating of wooden gongs, and the pounding of the derua (a large bamboo tube) against the ground. The dancers wear kilts of grass and leaves, circlets of leaves and flowers round the shoulders, necks, arms, and ankles, and a mask of soot painted around the eyes and on the centre of the forehead. The leader wears a broad tapa sash over his grass skirt, and a band of tapa diagonally across the chest and the left shoulder.

He leads his group, all armed with clubs and spears, through the ritual postures and gestures that used to be the prelude to battle. As the rhythm intensifies, and is punctuated by the hoarse *Hah! Hah! Hah!* of the warriors, and the stamping of their leather-hard feet on the ground, their eyes flash savagely through their black masks and their broad chests swell with a pulsing excitement which usually brings a nervous titter from the audience. It is possible to sense a faint echo of the ancient Fijian love of war for its own sake;

the primitive male delight in aggression. The Fijians no longer take to each other with spears and clubs, but under the discipline of modern warfare have proved their fighting spirit during the Pacific war against the Japanese and against the guerrillas during the Malaysian emergency.

The mekes danced by Fijian women are gentler and more graceful, and symbolize themes associated with domestic and village life or the planting and gathering of crops. Fijian women are always modestly dressed, usually in ankle-length skirts and long blouses which are a shapely adaptation of the missionaries' Mother Hubbards, and for their dances they add a flaring tapa skirt and decorations of hibiscus flowers and leaves. Sometimes they dance a kind of hula, imported from the Polynesian island of Rotuma which lies to the north of Fiji and comes under the Fijian government. It has a swaying, languorous movement, without the erotic overtones of the Hawaiian variety.

Women dancing a Meke

Fijian musical instruments include the lali; a drum made from a hollow log. Great skill and patience is needed in making a lali, because the log is hollowed out through a long, narrow aperture not much wider than a man's hand. It is beaten with short wooden clubs, and in the old days the thunder of the lali would summon men to war or to a council of the tribe. Nowadays it is used by some churches to call the faithful to prayer, and by some hotels to call the tourists to dinner, but the art and privilege of beating the lali is still jealously guarded.

Even more jealously preserved is the secret of the firewalkers, which has so far baffled all investigators. The firewalkers are members of the Sawau tribe, which lives in four villages on the island of Beqa. They give a demonstration from time to time, and one was witnessed in the Botanical Gardens at Suva.

A pit twelve feet across was filled with large stones, on which a log fire burned for several hours. When the stones had reached white heat, the firewalkers used sapling poles to pry aside the burning logs, and levelled the stones with a tree-fern trunk and a long, thick vine. All preparations were made with ritual care, and accompanied by a loud, dramatic chant.

The Bete, leader of the firewalkers, jumped onto the stones to test their firmness, and then ordered bundles of leaves and grass to be placed round the pit. When this had been done, the men who had prepared the firepit stood in a circle around it, leaving a gap for the firewalkers. These had remained behind some bushes, but now emerged to file through the guardians and onto the stones. As they walked over them they gave a sudden loud cry, and the bundles of leaves and grass were tossed onto the stones. The firewalkers congregated in the centre of the pit, chanting strongly, and at last returned onto the lawns. Relaxed, and smoking cigarettes, they allowed the bystanders to inspect their feet. They were unmarked, although a cotton handkerchief thrown onto the stones flared up immediately and crumpled into ash.

The firewalkers must observe strict taboos when preparing for the ceremony, and failure to do so may rob them of the power to walk on the stones unharmed. They must remain segregated from women for two weeks before the ceremony, and avoid eating coconut.

The legend of the firewalking tribe says that, long ago, the warrior Tui-na-Iviqalita promised a famous storyteller that he would make him a present of whatever he caught while fishing. He caught an eel, but when this was landed it transformed itself into a little man whom Tui recognized to be a spirit god.

The little man pleaded to be set free, and offered all kinds of gifts of which the most tempting was immunity from fire. He commanded the first firewalker's pit to be dug, leapt onto the white-hot stones, and invited Tui to join him. Tui obeyed, and found that the fire could not harm him. The god told him that, to gain complete mastery over fire, he must be buried in an earth oven for four days, but Tui was content with having risked his feet.

It is said that the Bete, the traditional high priests of the firewalkers, are directly descended from Tui-na-Iviqualita,

and that they inherit his ability to walk on fire and to lead others to follow them. So far, there has been no other explanation.

A similar legend concerns the strange ability of some Fijians to speak to the creatures of the sea. Today, the maidens of Namuana can sit on a clifftop and chant traditional songs, causing giant turtles to rise to the surface of the bay and loll gently on the surface as though listening to the music. These turtles are presumed to be descendants of two women who changed into turtles to escape from men of Nabukelevu, a village whose inhabitants were ancient enemies of Namuana. The two women, the wife and daughter of the Namuana chief, were fishing on a reef when a war canoe appeared. It was full of men from Nabukelevu, who seized and bound the women and threw them into the bottom of the canoe. But the gods of the sea came to the rescue, and a violent storm arose. The terrified men saw that the women had changed into turtles, and tossed them overboard. The turtles swam off towards Namuana, the storm subsided, and the men of Nabukelevu dug in their paddles and hurried away for home.

As proof of this story, the people of Namuana say that it is no use singing to the turtles if there are any men from Nabukelevu hanging around. The turtles still do not trust them.

322 ISLANDS?

Someone must know how many islands there are in the Fiji group, but it is hard to obtain an official estimate. One contact said warily, "It depends what you call an island." Another man said that you could name any figure between 300 and 500. Yet another informant stated emphatically that there are 322 islands. In any case, only about 100 islands have permanent inhabitants. Many of the others are called islands only by courtesy, and are simply rock and coral outcrops on which a few shrubs and coconut palms have taken root. Others lack fresh water, or are too isolated to attract inhabitants—although they may be visited by parties of Fijians who go there to fish or collect coconuts. If you are seeking a tropic island on which to retreat from civilization, you could certainly find one in Fiji—though the government looks with a jaundiced eye on anyone who attempts to live the life of a beachcomber.

The main islands are Viti Levu and Vanua Levu, and near to these are the smaller but still substantial islands of Taveuni, Koro, Bau, Ovalau, Kadavu, Beqa, and Vatulele. Between and around these lie many smaller islands, and the sharp-fanged reefs which were dreaded by early navigators—especially since a crowd of hungry Fijians would be waiting for any survivors from a wreck. The Lau Islands, where Tongan influence is still strong, lie to the south-east. The Yasawa and Mamanuca chains of islands, which recently have been discovered by tourists, lie to the north and north-west. Rotuma, which is not Fijian at all, lies about 300 miles to the north. Despite this distance it is administered by the Crown Colony of Fiji, and its people have become closely involved with Fijian affairs.

The whole group sprawls over a quarter of a million square

miles of sea. Uncounted centuries ago, this sea must have boiled with the eruption of a huge complex of volcanoes, bursting up from the sea-bed in a tumult of molten rock. This is now frozen into the steep mountains of the main islands, whose rugged green skyline is punctuated with frequent thrusting outcrops of naked stone. Sharp, dramatic pillars of rock, often in the form of natural citadels and watchtowers, are characteristic of some smaller islands such as the Yasawa group, but the legendary tropic island formation of palm-fringed beaches surrounding a sleepy lagoon can also be seen. Although its harsh contours are softened by the profuse green of jungle and rain-forest, the geography of Fiji is basically as primitive as the nature of its vanished cannibal tribes.

As always, geography dictates the weather. On the main islands, the mountains stand like a wall against the passage of the south-easterly trade winds, which blow great bulging rain clouds in from the Pacific. From November to March, these clouds spill enormous quantities of rain onto the south-eastern slopes of the islands, and cause them to grow green and fertile. But the mountains prevent the rainstorms from passing completely over the land, and neatly divide the islands into wet and dry zones. So the northern slopes and shores are comparatively brown and arid in appearance, and present a sunbaked contrast to the opulent fertility of the

south. From the air, the line of demarcation can be seen as clearly as though it were drawn on a map.

In the rainy season, the rain descends with a massive authority, and a first experience of such tropical rainstorms can be almost alarming. It is heralded by a dull, distant roar, increasing with ominous speed, and making the newcomer think that he is in the path of one of Fiji's rare hurricanes. Then there is the sharp insistence of the first raindrops striking the iron roofs, and swiftly rising to a deafening crescendo. It passes as abruptly as it came, to be followed by an abrupt, eerie silence broken only by the sound of water dripping from the eaves and the palm trees swishing in the wind.

Fiji lies within the Pacific hurricane belt, and occasionally the islands are victims of frenzied winds and rainstorms. Their effects are intensified by the way in which the water cascades down the mountainside, to swell the rivers and cause them to flood with terrifying rapidity. Fijian rivers, though comparatively short, carry a great volume of water, and before the days of motor vehicles were the most important highways.

Despite their basic similarity, some of the hundreds of Fijian islands have unique features. Many Fijians believe

Island of Sawa-i-Lau

the most beautiful island to be Taveuni, whose special feature is a freshwater lake in the crater of an extinct volcano. The shores of this lake have some peculiar property that allows them to grow the lovely Tagimaucia flower, which cannot be grown anywhere else on the island. The flower is used in island ceremonies, and a gift of a floral decoration made of Tagimaucia is regarded as a high honour.

Sawa-i-Lau Island is distinguished by its dramatic silhouette, because it has a dominant central mass of rock flanked by two low-lying wings of land. Seen from afar, it

Pictographic writing at entrance to cave on Sawa-i-Lau

seems like a great bird resting on the clear waters of the Pacific. The island is also remarkable for a great cave and an underground lake, and cut into the rock at the entrance to the cave are pictographic symbols which are believed to be of Mongolian origin, and at least 3,000 years old. Prehistoric stone axe-heads have been found near to the cave.

Yalobi village, on the island shore, occupies a spectacular position between a grove of coconut palms, a fine sandy beach, and a towering pillar of rock. This pillar casts a striking reflection on the water, and must have been a useful watchtower in the old days of sea-raiders.

Communications between and within the islands range from the old seaways, once travelled by war parties in canoes which an early visitor said could do better than twenty knots under sail, to the skyways used by Fiji Airways. The air service was founded by Harold Gatty, the Tasmanian who flew as navigator with Wiley Post on the first round-world flight in 1931, and it now connects most of the main centres of the islands as well as flying to other Pacific Island groups. The aircraft usually fly at comparatively low altitudes, and an inter-island flight provides some memorable visual experiences. Great clouds cast vast reflections on the sea, and distant islands float like vague silhouettes on the far horizon where the sea meets the sky in a blurred diffusion of colour. Coral reefs resemble web-like tentacles spreading beneath the surface of the sea, and the varying depths of water show up as vivid aquatones of phosphorescent green

Drover aircraft of Fiji Airways.

and turquoise, with deep pits of primary blues, cobalts, and ultramarines.

Flying over the land, you can look down into valleys filled with a green foam of jungle, laced with the red threads of earthen roads passing through villages whose thatched roofs are the colour of dry grass. The palms of coconut plantations cast slender shadows, and the still water glints in flooded rice-fields. On the northern slopes of the islands there are neat blocks of vivid green cut by straight roads or winding rail tracks; the plantations of sugar cane, which grows best on the drier northern side.

The Fijians inherit an ancient tradition of seamanship, and the masters of the little ketches, schooners, and power craft which ply between the islands can follow the sea-tracks as confidently as a man driving along a well-known road. A lifelong association with the waters surrounding their islands has made them familiar with the reefs and shoals and the pattern of the currents; the shapes of natural features which act as landmarks to isolated harbours, and the significance of almost imperceptible changes in the weather. There is a romantic aura about the little ships tied up alongside in Suva or sailing along the green coastline of one of the outer islands, and they are somehow reminiscent of the bad old days when such ships were loaded with a cargo of trade

goods, with which to tempt Pacific islanders to a life of toil in the canefields of Queensland. But nowadays they are strictly businesslike . . . though it is romantic enough to read that they are bound for such places as the Koro Sea and the Lomaiviti Islands. Those who have the time to spare can travel as passengers on such a voyage, but must be prepared for hard lying and a vigorous motion. By way of compensation for such discomforts, there is an opportunity to see the solitary beauty of uninhabited islands, and to land at friendly little villages where the arrival of the ship is a momentous event.

Evidence of one of the sea's classic mysteries can be seen in the hull of the *Joyita*, rotting on the beach near Levuka. Built in 1931 as a pleasure yacht for a Hollywood tycoon, the little vessel had a history of ill-fortune which culminated in a voyage from Apia to Tokelau in 1955. Nearly two months after leaving Apia, the *Joyita* was found drifting and abandoned, about 167 miles off Vanua Levu. She was towed into Suva, but no trace of her twenty-five passengers and crew has ever been found. She was sold to a copra planter, and sent to sea again, but ran aground twice and was finally beached at Levuka.

Some of the little ships go as far as Rotuma, the Polynesian island which is in the nature of a dependency of Fiji. Only about eight miles long and two miles wide, it is a lush, fertile island which was once a haven for adventurers of the South Seas. Many of them died violently from quarrels amongst themselves or with the islanders, and rival Christian missions added to the confusion. At one period, Catholics and Protestants fought each other as enthusiastically as they now do in Belfast, and eventually the island chiefs solved the problem by giving their island to Fiji in the same way that Fiji was given to Britain. The Rotuma islanders make singularly fine handicrafts, and their baskets and mats show an even greater creative ability than that of the Fijians.

Even inland travel in Fiji smacks of the sea, because a vehicle must swoop and curvet over the steep, winding roads with all the tail-wagging abandon of a ketch in a fresh breeze. Outside the towns, the roads are very rough, and tend to become slithering mud-tracks during the rainy seasons. But the drivers of the buses which connect the villages treat these

The Joyita

conditions with great aplomb, and accelerate down precipitous lanes, so narrow that the undergrowth whips the sides of the vehicles, as though they were driving along a freeway. The buses are well kept and operate punctually to timetable, but instead of window-glass they have canvas blinds. Kept furled in dry weather, they are rolled down when it rains, and this makes the interior steamy and claustrophobic—especially when travelling at high speed along a winding country road, with your view of the outside world restricted to glimpses through a windscreen smeared with mud and rain.

Passengers on country buses carry anything from chickens and fresh-caught fish to baskets of fruit and vegetables, and they are a chatty and friendly crowd. No standing passengers are allowed, but there seems to be no rule against people sitting on the floor. The arrival of the bus is often the big daily event in the life of villagers, for whom it provides the main link with the outside world. It brings their groceries, newspapers, and fresh bread, together with the latest gossip from other villages.

The villages are often as isolated amongst the jungle as the islands are isolated in the sea. They are approached by rough roads which wind through areas of dense jungle and rain forest, with thick clusters of bamboo and high palm trees, and occasional clearings where such vegetables as dalo are grown. In the wet season, veils of misty cloud hang low over the slopes, and the rain causes visibility to be even more restricted in the dense tangle of green. This is "Tarzan country," without the apes and other wild animals, and vines as thick as ropes hang amongst the fleshy leaves of muscular, thick-trunked trees. There is a feeling of writhing fecundity struggling for space, air, and sunlight, and with no room for humanity.

The Fijians are flower-lovers, and some of the flowering shrubs which grow so profusely, under ideal conditions of soil and humidity, have a ceremonial significance as well as being used for everyday decoration. The hibiscus, in all its varied brilliance, has attained the status of a national flower. Vermilion and crimson poinsettias and flamboyants are worn by war-dancing warriors as well as by village maidens. The delicately shaped frangipanis are woven into sweet-smelling necklaces. All such flowers grow wild, as well as in suburban gardens.

The forests also provide a wealth of useful timbers, with such mellifluous names as ewe, dakua, kauvala, vesi, rosawa, and saro-saro. In the past, only the most casual attention was needed to grow food-bearing trees, including the breadfruit

Palms in Suva

Bread Fruit tree

which brought Captain Bligh's ill-fated expedition into the South Seas, and coconut palms, paw-paws, mangoes and bananas all flourish—but have to combat pests which have been imported from other islands.

It was this exuberant fertility that encouraged the white man to bring an exotic vegetation to Fiji. This was sugar; cousin to the grass and bamboo. It was to transform Fiji's economy and ecology, and cause the islands to become host to a new race which has now lived there long enough to regard Fiji as its home.

Tree trunks: the beach at Nasilai

SUGAR AND SIVA

Degei, the serpent-god of the ancient Fijians, has long since vanished into the jungle whence he was conjured by the priests, who also worshipped the spirits of departed chiefs and heroes and sacrificed human offerings to ensure success in war and other affairs. Modern Fijians are Christians, and most of them adhere to the Methodist faith which was brought to them by the first missionaries. But Christmas and Easter are not the only religious festivals celebrated on the islands, and many of the inhabitants follow other paths in the eternal search for truth. Holi, the spring festival of the Hindus, fills the streets with gay crowds of Indians who squirt each other with coloured water, and later in the year they deck their homes with lights in order to welcome Lakshmi, the goddess of prosperity. Brahma the creator, Vishnu the preserver, and Siva the destroyer are as significant to the Hindus as Guru Nanak is to the Sikhs, or Allah and Mohammed to the Muslims. These three great religions of India flourish in Fiji, because the islands contain more Indians than Fijians.

Indians have lived there for almost a century, but their forebears would have little in common with their confident and industrious descendants. They were brought to Fiji because the first exploiters of the land had to provide themselves with cheap labour, and found a bottomless reservoir in the poverty-stricken masses of India.

The first white settlers contented themselves with such products as were readily available; first sandalwood, then coconuts and turtleshell. The American Civil War, which caused a world shortage of cotton, inspired the growing of this commodity and attracted more settlers. These may have thought that the islanders would perform all the tedious

Roman Catholic Mission near Lautoka, Island of Ovalau

work of land-clearing, cultivation, and harvesting, but soon found that the intelligent Fijians were disinclined to labour for another's gain. So the planters imported workers from the Solomon Islands and the New Hebrides, until the outcry against "blackbirding" put a stop to this traffic.

It ended at about the same time as the collapse of the cotton boom, but before that some planters had tried their hands at sugar-growing. It flourished in the fertile soil, and (since the white man was convinced that heavy toil in the tropics would be the death of him) the only problem was that of sufficient coloured labour to do the work.

So the first shipload of Indians was recruited, and brought to Fiji in 1879. They were bluntly known as "coolies," and imported under an indenture system which bound them for five years to the planters, obliged them to stay in the islands for a further five years, and would then repatriate them if they so desired. Before the indenture system ended, in 1919, more than 60,000 Indians had been brought to Fiji. Less than

half of them returned home, and those who remained have multiplied so greatly that the Indian population of Fiji is now over 250,000 . . . despite the fact that, in the indenture days, only forty Indian women could accompany every hundred men.

The coolie system reflects no credit upon those which employed it. Theoretically, the Indians were recruited under regulations which at least had regard for their basic human rights. In fact, they were treated as little better than creatures which had two legs to walk on and two arms to swing a cane-knife or hoe. Most of the Indians were Hindus, a creed which is stratified into a rigid caste system. Each caste believes that it is contaminated, in a religious sense, by contact with people of an inferior degree. But the planters paid no heed to such niceties, and every caste, from the Brahmins of the hereditary priesthood to the Untouchables who were hereditary scavengers, was lumped together in the transports. They were further intermingled in the "Lines"

Indian Farmer

of coolie hutments, in which they were accommodated on the plantations. They were treated with imperial contempt by their European overseers, and discouraged from association with the Fijians—who also looked down upon them.

These conditions, which were made worse by the heavy seasonal labour and the disproportion of the sexes, caused a simmering resentment which from time to time erupted into strikes, riots, murders, suicides, and wife-stealing.

But Indians have survived many centuries of natural disasters and human oppression, and, like the sugar-cane which they had been imported to attend, they found that the soil of Fiji was one in which they could flourish. Many of them, when released from servitude to the plantations, had saved enough of their wages to rent a little piece of land from Fijian tribes which had plenty to spare. They began farming in a small way, and by dawn-to-dusk labour they made their farms succeed. But the real turning of the tables came in 1920.

Until then, most Fijian sugar had been grown on huge estates which belonged to a few large companies. These companies had secured ownership of large tracts of land, although, since the Cession of the islands, it has been difficult for individuals to buy Fijian land. Most of it is held in trust for the tribes, of which it is the communal property, or for the Crown. Land can be rented, but not purchased.

When the indenture system ended, labour problems began. The great estates were gradually broken up into small holdings, and nowadays the greater part of the cane is grown on farms which are usually only about ten acres in extent—and which are held by Indians. Most of the money earned by the primary production of sugar goes to Indian families; the descendants of men and women who were told that Fiji was "somewhere near Calcutta," and who were driven to emigrate into bondage by the hopelessness of their native conditions.

Like Australians and Americans, who are developing into peoples very different from those who first settled their nations, the Fijian Indians have their own characteristics. Their frank gaze and confident movements are a sharp

contrast to the toilworn condition of many mainland Indians. Their natural industry and resourcefulness have enabled them to develop freely; not only as farmers, but as shopkeepers, businessmen, mechanics, doctors, and in many other occupations including the law, because there are few things which Indians enjoy better than a lengthy lawsuit. The children and teenagers are physically attractive, with straight slender bodies and a proud, striding walk; attributes which show the effects of an ample diet as well as that of growing up in a free and expansive community. Many of them are well educated, because the Indians maintain their own excellent schools, and nowadays the students can go on to the recently-established University of Fiji. Some of these will find executive careers in the public service, administering the country in which Indians were once regarded as little better than slaves. Others may even help to govern the islands, because Fiji is ruled by a Legislative Assembly somewhat similar to that of Papua-New Guinea, with most of the members being elected out of the indigenous population.

The Indians, whether Hindus, Muslims, or Sikhs, are evident in almost every phase of Fijian life; giving it their own accents of colour from the brightly-dyed sweetmeats of the kerbside vendors to the somewhat garish ornamentation of a rich man's bungalow; from the saris which Indian girls can wear with such exquisite flair to the shop windows crammed with a parrot-bright display of imported merchandise.

Ironically, the forced intermingling of the castes, which was so much resented by the first emigrants, has had a beneficial effect. It broke the rigid tyranny of the caste system, so that the present generation has lost much of the old intra-religious prejudice. But there are still tensions within the Indian community. These are not apparent when one sees a group of young Indians swinging golf clubs over land on which their forebears might have swung cane knives, but they do exist. They are largely caused by the fact that the Indians, who make up more than half of the population, own very little of the land on which they work. They can rent it, but rarely can they buy it. Agitators whip up trouble from time to time, and throw various other bones of contention into the resulting dogfight. There was a big one in 1960, when Indian sugar-growers refused to supply the company-owned mills with cane. Stand-over tactics were used against those who would not join the strike, and dissentients were awoken by the crackle of their canefields going up in flames. The Government had to use force to cram the lid back on the simmering kettle of resentment. So long as the Indians continue to win the population race, while regarding themselves as being the subjects of discrimination, then discontent is inevitable. It is not fair to draw a "Black Power" parallel, but the observer cannot help thinking in that direction . . . and hoping that Siva the destroyer will not prove to be the most potent force in future politics.

The rights and wrongs of the coolie system, and the company ownership of land, are still the subject of endless discussion over the curry-bowl. But the Colonial Sugar Refining Co., the only survivor of the great sugar companies of the past, pursues an enlightened programme of research, training, and organization. It spends largely on such services as weed-control and cane-breeding, advises the smallholders on how to get the best out of their land, and maintains a complete railway system with which it helps the farmers to transport their cane to the mills. "So they ought," is no doubt the reaction of the agitators, but an industry as huge and important as Fijian sugar must certainly benefit by this kind of overall control.

Since the 1880s, sugar has been the most significant Fiji industry, and has played the main part in the economic development of the islands. It was first grown in the wet southern areas, until it was discovered that cane grown on the dry northern sectors was higher in sugar content. The water-catching southern slopes have proved to be ideal for the growing of rice, and the Indians are adept at raising this traditional food of their race. The Fijians relish rice, but for some reason do not care to grow it—perhaps because their

hearty and extrovert natures are not suited to the finicking process of rice cultivation.

But the Fijians have a long agricultural history, and were using bamboo pipes to irrigate their fields before Captain Cook entered the Pacific. Their lands, being communally held, were also worked on a communal basis, and in some areas it is still the practice for the villagers to assemble every morning and wait for the chief to decide upon the work for the day. Proceeds from the leasing of communal land, and from a tax or "cess" on coconut production, are used for such village improvements as housing and water-supply.

Nowadays, their main money crops are coconuts and bananas, and they have a monopoly on the latter fruit. Much of their produce is exported to New Zealand. Coconuts are also a "wet-side" crop, and are grown in plantations ranging from small family affairs up to large company-owned establishments. Most of the coconut meat is dried into copra, and a ketch coming in from one of the outer islands with a cargo of copra has a ripe and fruity smell. Most of it goes to Europe and Japan, and ends as soap or margarine.

Lautoka Harbour scene

Copra Estate

Tobacco is another long-established Fijian crop, and it is often sold as "twist" which looks like a coil of dark-brown lanyard. Ten cents will buy about four inches, but it is a hardy smoker who will take more than a few puffs after filling his pipe with the local brand.

The first Europeans settled in Fiji during the era when most newly-discovered countries were optimistically explored in search for gold. A persistent rumour about Fijian gold managed to survive geologists' reports that the landforms made it unlikely, and in 1929 the first strike was made in the south of Vanua Levu. A Suva merchant staked an old prospector to look for gold on Viti Levu, and by the early 1930s he was digging out gold in the north of that island. This turned out to be the first strike on the rich Tavua field, and led to the discovery of three considerable gold mines. As always, gold acted as a magnet to men from all over the world, and there was a brief gold-rush which petered out after a year or two, when it was realized that the precious metal was limited to the areas in which claims had been staked. The peak producing year was 1947, when 134,922 ounces earned nearly three million dollars for the mines, but in the years since then the production has averaged less than 100,000 ounces annually and profits have been restricted by the international pegging of gold prices.

Some other minerals are found in the Fijian Islands, especially manganese, and there are some other primary industries such as timber-milling and the collecting of trochus shells for the sake of their mother-of-pearl.

Sturdy little Japanese fishing craft take tuna from the surrounding waters, and call in at Suva with rows of sharks' tails drying on their decks and advertising their presence along the wharves, but fishing has not developed into anything more than a domestic industry. Sugar is still the lord of the islands, and the rum-like aroma of molasses hangs heavily over such towns as Lautoka and Ba during the crushing season.

Coconut Palm

Timber Mill, Deuba

Sugar, during the nineteenth century, revolutionized the islands in countless ways, great and small; from the introduction of Indian labour to the introduction of the Indian mongoose, brought in to deal with snakes among the cane and later developing an appetite for native birds. It opened up the country with roads and small-gauge railways—of which the best-known example is the railway which carries tourists from Lautoka waterfront into the township—and despite the undulations of world sugar-prices it is still the backbone of the island economy.

But in this century a new industry is bringing a new revolution. The industry is tourism, which since the late 1950s has brought many thousands of visitors to Fiji. The islands have always attracted cruise-ships and holiday-makers, but were far enough off the beaten track to make them a comparatively exotic holiday destination. The development of international air travel changed all that, and Fiji became a stopover point for trans-Pacific flights. Nadi, the airfield established by New Zealand forces in 1939 and later extended by the Americans, was ideal for the big passenger aircraft, and it was soon realized that it could be a gateway for the profitable tourist traffic. Travel agents in Australia, New Zealand and the United States developed the "package tour," which for one all-inclusive fare provided return travel to Fiji and accommodation and travel within the islands, and the Fiji Government encouraged tourism by special loans and concessions and the establishment of the Fiji Visitors Bureau. There is now a year-round flow of visitors into Fiji, even during the wet season when special economy terms are offered.

No one can foretell the final result. So far, it has been good. The visitors inject a formidable amount of cash into the Fijian economy, and its effects are enjoyed by many islanders; from the basket weavers in the markets to the owners of the big new hotels. The tourist is welcomed with typical Fijian friendliness, which makes him feel that he may be more welcome than his money. When the sightseeing buses stop at a Fijian village, the children flock out to meet the visitors

Hotel Lounge

VITI JEWELLERS
ISLAND CURIOS
&
FANCY GOODS

with an eager excitement, and the Indian shopkeepers maintain a smiling patience towards the people who paw through their goods and sometimes treat them with a suspicious discourtesy. It is a good place to visit, because the sense of hospitality is strong.

Times have changed since Cakobau appealed for protection against the "stalkers on the beach," and the ships docking at Lautoka disgorge hordes of well-fed tourists instead of dazed coolies from the slums and villages of India. The Fijians no longer appraise newcomers with an eye to their succulence, and the war-dance is debased into night-club entertainment. Even greater changes must lie ahead, and it is to be hoped that such changes will not affect the beauty of the islands nor the friendliness of their people.

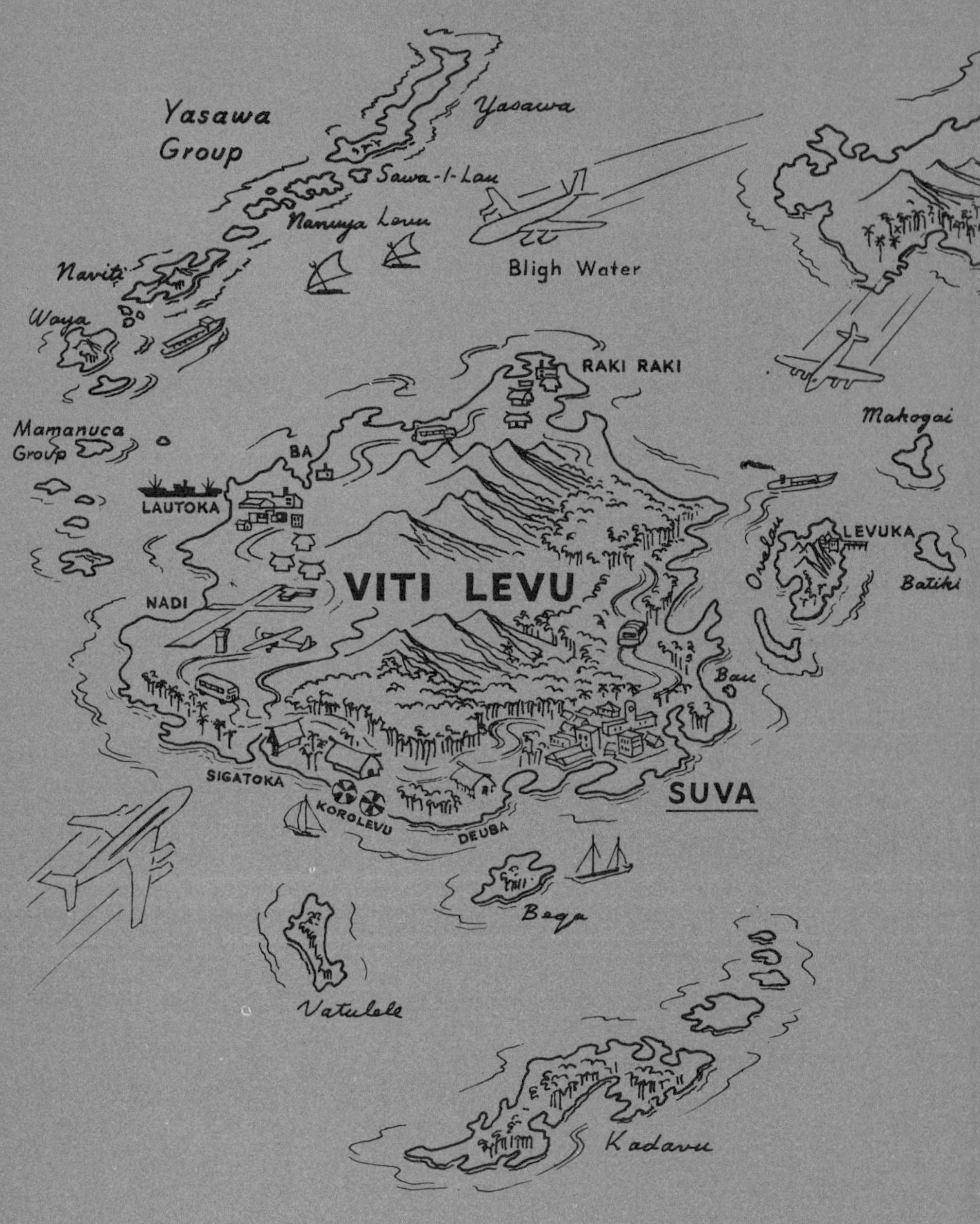
Yasawa
Group
Yasawa
Sawa-I-Lau
Nanuya Levu
Bligh Water
Naviti
Waya
RAKI RAKI
Makogai
Mamanuca
Group
BA
LAUTOKA
LEVUKA
Ovalau
Batiki
VITI LEVU
NADI
Bau
SIGATOKA
SUVA
KOROLEVU
DEUBA
Beqa
Vatulele
Kadavu